One Oh One

Leah Georgie Joy

BookLeaf Publishing

Presentation by *BookLeaf Publishing*

Web: www.bookleafpub.com

E-mail: info@bookleafpub.com

ISBN: 9789358311839

First edition 2023

For Caleb

ACKNOWLEDGEMENT

One Oh One owes everything to the incredible people in my life. It was a mad rush to put together in 21 days, so thank you for those who supported my madness: Caleb, my romaence paertner; my mother and father (if you saw me write "cunt" in this book, no you didn't); my siblings, Hannah and Kaiden; the Humble Creative Collective; Kimmy Joy, who undertook this with me and created the remarkable This is Where I Live Now; and of course, my two garbage baby cats.

Dandelioness

My sister's favorite flower is a weed,
crossing miles with short-shallow roots,
cracking sidewalk concrete
and performing kintsugi
with its gold.

She's on the night shift
at the hospital, so I leave a voicemail:

"Do you remember?
We licked each other's wounds
first?
I taste
the blood.
Were we quick enough
to learn
that girlhood is violence?

I leave another:
"I made a wish
blowing on a dandelion
today."

I Never Run for the Bus

The best seat on the 14R is currently occupied
by a toddler, her small soft
fist curled around the first
stolen poppy of the spring.

The best seat on the 14R is currently occupied
by a crushed poppy, left behind,
a shame or a gift. Or
fallen from a small soft fist
that never felt scarcity in beauty.

Ode to the Pigeon

My little half-tamed
beast of burdens since lifted.
What do you carry?

Crumbs of sourdough,
bits of newspaper to nest,
the shadow of doves.

Your iridescent
moonstone throat, a lonely coo
deadened by our noise.

In every urban toxic hole,
you see the shoes, you see the soul.

Crocker Avenue

Who among the residents of Crocker Avenue
will come to claim the body
of the raccoon?
Who will stroke the soft fur under her chin,
and take her from the blistering pavement,
lose their security deposit
digging a hole in borrowed earth?
Will they whisper a eulogy
too small for the family dog, or
beg a cross
from the Korean church up the hill?
Or
on their long and hazy commute, will they say
"Give her a moment longer
to stare up at the stars
and the Fourth of July fireworks."

The Littlest Redwood

I sit astride
like I'd ride a pony, saddled
with Joan Didion and
a cold summer
tomato sandwich, salted,
in crinkling parchment.
Cars do not stop in their migration
across the last road that does not spit dust.

Tomorrow I will come back.
I'll lie in the lee
empty of hand,
trying not to begrudge the love
of earthworms and mushrooms by
pretending I am Earth–I do not recognize.
the sound of engines sputtering through
the city's last oasis of dirt.

She Says My Work is Growing Legs

If my poem grew legs, it would just flail
into the world while it sleeps, kicking
against nonexistence, then rise
on shaking knobby knees like a
foal born in a field in April.
It would learn to run and frolick
til its shins were skinned and bruised.
Its feet would ache beautifully
by the end of a long day of quickness.
It would go bare into the brambles daily
and never scab or grow a thicker skin.
It would develop restless pains at night
deep in its poem hamstrings, then sleepwalk
out of my home and catch the next bus out.

I couldn't stop it if I tried.
But I don't think I would try.

Shortcuts

I think the monsters of the Midwest
would be my friends
now. If
something crawled out from
under my bed, at least it wouldn't
be empty.

I think The Thing From The Closet
in my parents' house would take
my face in its needle and sandpaper paws
and say,

One day you'll look down
and see the slick rocks on the pier
under your scraped-pink toes again.
You'll smell The Lake Michigan Kelp Kreature
and she will
protect you from
The Beastie That Stalks the Soybean Field,
and he will
protect you from
The Great Leviathan Under The Gravel Pit,
and

you will be so glad
to fear us again.

Scribbles

My mother's voice on the phone
asks if I miss the weather
–I don't, but–
(yes, it's fifty-five and cloudy)
(yes, again, but)
I miss talking about the weather
with strangers caught in a downpour,
children frying an egg on chalked-up pavement,
dads standing by the grill, watching for
a whisper of a storm to roll by
til someone says "We really needed that."

My mother's voice says if
I keep picking the scab on my jaw
it will leave a scar, even though,
you know,
she can't see it.
Her voice asks if I have any new tattoos.
(no, but I'd like to)
(no, they aren't enough like scars)
–I don't say that, but–
Her voice asks if I know those scribbles are
permanent.
Something has to be.

Seven Ways to Wear a Problem

On my sleeve, a peek
of hand-loomed lace,
long, to cover cracked knuckles,
leaving only fingertips
Exposed as a knockoff, bought
half price from a near stranger
on my street, at least
to the average eye it looks
Real, vintage, my mother's
in the eighties,
look how it fits!
She's got these skinny hips
Too expensive, from overseas,
the latest in Milan, I'm told
–looked better on the model–
but
Still as I can stay
to avoid being pricked with pins,
getting it tailored,
ripping and re-sewing all the
Stitches dropped, unraveling yarn
It's my first project, I lack
the callouses for the knitting needles,
can't count, lost my

Place in the sun to dry so
it won't shrink by accident.
They don't make these like
They used to
rub blisters into my flesh, but
I've broken them in now.

Intermission

I come from a long line of people
who need to sit close to the exit

Did I Read the Book?

Mrs. Dalloway said she would buy
the flowers herself–
opium poppies, imported–
Said she would call the pharmacy herself,
practicing pronunciation–
"dylar" said like a clandestine fuck.
Said she would eat dripping oranges in the
shower
by herself, dry herself
off and smother her skin in Alo Glo
til positively radioactive
Said, "you better fix my life, you little shit"
to a dinner of ice-nine
Tucked herself into silk sheets like poppy petals
whispered
cunt
in her most secret voice
whispered
"I am not an apology."

Molehills

He says I am so good
at making something out of nothing.
I say, you loved that once.

You could follow the scent
of a festering heart, even
when I disappeared
round the corner, into the woods.
You knew
I'd never learn, never take
root in the great apathy of nature–
it wasn't mine.

Don't Ever Call Me Resilient

So I went to California
just to say I'm from Michigan–
tiptoe-on-the-barely-frozen-waves Michigan–
scrape-the-ice-off-your-windshield-with-your-ba
re-goddamn-hands Michigan–
fuck it, stick-your-head-out-the-window-where
-the-air-whips-your-face-to-ribbons-and
-hit-a-deer-anyway Michigan.

Forgive me if I crave hostility, if
I long to be rejected–
bruised like fruit, tossed down high hills
to the ocean that will salt my new wounds.

Long Distance Daughter

The breadcrumb trail I left you
is no grain of sustenance, I know.

How trained is the eye
when the stomach is empty?

I know the way is long, and us
in our teeth, bared
against the strangers
into which we may slip
by the end.

Fruh-NELL

I invented three excuses
to see you again, say
goodbye again,
"for real this time"
just because I was in the neighborhood,
just in case it is
"for real this time."

I think of sending you a picture
of a lighthouse, but I see
you're already inside.
Moments before
you pick me out of the tempest
with your Fresnel, I realize
the old wickie's warning:

Don't come home
lest ye dash your vessel
against the rocks
and waterlog your bones
but a wave away
from where they could have been
laid dry
in the sun
tomorrow.

It's Rotten Work

You take in the murder scene in the bathroom
and say, "chemical warfare
raspberry soda hair" "like
the song".

You lie me on the couch with
a lingering touch on my hair and hand
-feed me bits of starlight,
set me up with
an old episode of The Twilight Zone
and a strawberry right from the garden,
a shoebox in the garage
and an old roommate's headboard.
We'll use our shame as kindling
and let it burn low and slow
to ember
and soot
in the west
and stoke it up again
in the east.

Kimmy

The old crone says
when I see you again, our
Fates will have woven back to trinity
We'll have reached divinity, reading
two thousand road signs, scrying weeping
remains of the raccoon
you pass on the way to work
Text me a picture, say
"Still here"

$418 in My Bank Account

You do not have to buy
the good boots that will last.

You can walk in faux leather that leaks
to the corner store with the
small stale coffee and marked-up
cigarettes.

You can snuff them out half-
smoked, and watch the cloud rise
to join the fog
rolling in across the bay.

The End

In the end, the End
The End waited eighty years and found me,
nineteen or twenty, a little too drunk
leaving a party.
Stumbling to the gas station
where I told him to meet me.
There's a chill on the night air, even though
it's only September, and I forgot
my jacket and everything in its pockets and I'm
a little worried about
how I'll atone for my choices tonight
in this state of
spinning streetlights and kaleidoscopes of
familiar storefronts.

But the End pulls up in the old family Honda
and
gets out, and he
smiles a little.

"Did you have fun?" he asks.
"Yes," I say, even though I can't
quite remember it yet.

"Good. Let's go home."

P.S. (Or, I Leave Another)

I made a wish
blowing on a dandelion
today.
Willowy wisps of silver
evoked some wisdom above me, as though
I didn't arrive when it was just a bud.
A little soldier in time's march on.

www.ingramcontent.com/pod-product-compliance
Lightning Source LLC
LaVergne TN
LVHW050302200726

843509LV00015B/3115